Stories in ART

Sculpture

Richard Spilsbury

PowerKiDS press

New York

Published in 2009 by The Rosen Publishing Group Inc.
29 East 21st Street, New York, NY 10010

First Edition

Senior Editor: Claire Shanahan
Designer: Rachel Hamdi/Holly Fulbrook
Project Maker: Anna-Marie d'Cruz
Models: Rheanne Khokar, Alex Watson
Photographer: Andy Crawford

Library of Congress Cataloging-in-Publication Data

Spilsbury, Richard, 1963-
   Sculpture / Richard Spilsbury. — 1st ed.
      p. cm. — (Stories in art)
   Includes index.
   ISBN 978-1-4042-4435-1 (library binding)
   1. Sculpture—Juvenile literature. 2. Sculpture—Technique—Juvenile literature. I. Title.
   NB1143.S65 2009
   730—dc22
                                      2007052733

Title page, p14/15: AFP/Getty Images; p6: Scott Barbour/Getty Images; p7: Private Collection/ Photo ©
Heini Schneebeli/The Bridgeman Art Library; p8: © tradewinds/Alamy; p9: Museum of Fine Arts,
Houston, Texas, Agnes Cullen Arnold Endowment Fund/The Bridgeman Art Library; p10/11: © Carl &
Ann Purcell/Corbis; p12/13: Terracotta Army, Qin Dynasty, 210 BC; warriors (detail) by Tomb of Qin shi
Huang Di, Xianyang, China/The Bridgeman Art Library; p16/17, front cover: Tipu's Tiger, c.1790 (wood)
by Indian School, (eighteenth century), Victoria & Albert Museum, London, U.K./The Bridgeman Art
Library; p18/19: Raising the flag on Iwo Jima, U.S. Marine Corps Memorial, Arlington National Cemetery,
Washington, D.C. (photo) by American Photographer (twentieth century), Private Collection/ Peter
Newark Pictures/The Bridgeman Art Library; p20/21: Haida Eagle clan totem pole (painted wood) by
Canadian School, Private Collection/ Photo © Boltin Picture Library/The Bridgeman Art Library

Manufactured in China

Contents

What is sculpture?

A sculpture is a **three-dimensional** work of art. Three-dimensional means something that is not flat—it has height, width, and depth. Some sculptures can be viewed from all sides, and some are in relief—the form is **carved** or **modeled** from a flat background. Sculptures can be life-size, or much bigger or much smaller. Some sculptures are just for looking at or touching, but others are so big you can walk among or through them!

What are sculptures made from?

There are many different kinds of sculptures and a variety of different materials. Some sculptures are made from hard materials, such as wood, metal, and stone. Others could be made of anything, even ice, chocolate, or sand—so a sand castle on a beach could be described as a kind of sculpture!

Some sculptures are made from found or natural objects. Many sculptures are of people, but sculptures can be of anything, from animals to aircraft. Some sculptures are not realistic. They do not look like anything in particular, but express a feeling or mood instead.

◄ This is a giant sculpture of a table and chair made from steel and wood by the artist Giancarlo Neri. The people underneath are normal height adults!

History of sculpture

People have been making sculptures for thousands of years. Before people could write or leave written records of their lives and religious beliefs, sculptures were often used to tell stories or to act as **symbols** to represent something important. Stone Age people made statues and carvings of animals and people out of stone and ivory. On Easter Island, there are more than 600 huge, carved stone statues of big heads made around a thousand years ago. No one knows why they were made. Some sculptures are made to protect entrances, or to make a palace or public building look important, but other sculptures are purely decorative.

▶ *Some ancient sculptures have survived for centuries. This Greek statue of a goddess was carved from stone over 2,200 years ago.*

How to use this book

Background information on each sculpture featured, including its designer, date, location, and history

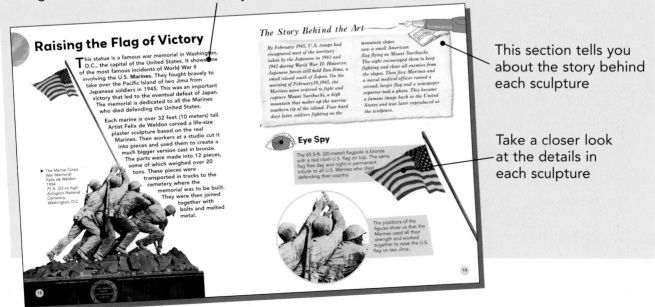

Raising the Flag of Victory

This statue is a famous war memorial in Washington, D.C., the capital of the United States. It shows one of the most famous incidents of World War II involving the U.S. **Marines**. They fought bravely to take over the Pacific Island of Iwo Jima from Japanese soldiers in 1945. This was an important victory that led to the eventual defeat of Japan. The memorial is dedicated to all the Marines who died defending the United States.

Each marine is over 32 feet (10 meters) tall. Artist Felix de Weldon carved a life-size plaster sculpture based on the real Marines. Then workers at a studio cut it into pieces and used them to create a much bigger version cast in bronze. The parts were made into 12 pieces, some of which weighed over 20 tons. These pieces were transported in trucks to the cemetery where the memorial was to be built. They were then joined together with bolts and melted metal.

▶ The Marine Corps War Memorial Felix de Weldon 1954 75 ft. (23 m) high Arlington National Cemetery, Washington, D.C.

The Story Behind the Art

By February 1945, U.S. troops had recaptured most of the territory taken by the Japanese in 1941 and 1942 during World War II. However, Japanese forces still held Iwo Jima, a small island south of Japan. On the morning of February 19, 1945, the Marines were ordered to fight and capture Mount Suribachi, a high mountain that makes up the narrow southern tip of the island. Four hard days later, soldiers fighting on the mountain slopes saw a small American flag flying on Mount Suribachi. The sight encouraged them to keep fighting and clear all enemies from the slopes. Then five Marines and a naval medical officer raised a second, larger flag and a newspaper reporter took a photo. This became a famous image back in the United States and was later reproduced as the sculpture.

Eye Spy

The 65.5-ft. (20-meter) flagpole is bronze with a real cloth U.S. flag on top. The same flag flies day and night in permanent tribute to all U.S. Marines who died defending their country.

The positions of the figures show us that the Marines used their strength and worked together to raise the U.S. flag on Iwo Jima.

This section tells you about the story behind each sculpture

Take a closer look at the details in each sculpture

How are sculptures made?

Sculptures are made in a variety of ways. Here are four main methods.

▲ *This sculptor is hammering a sharp chisel against a stone block to carve the shape of a dog's head.*

Carving

In carving, the artist cuts from a block of solid material to create a sculpture. Sculptures are often carved from marble, other stone, or wood. Artists use tools such as hammers and chisels. Some wood carvers carve sculptures from wood using chainsaws. Larger pieces are cut off in chunks and then details are added by careful chiseling and scraping. Sometimes artists carve softer materials, such as soap and ice.

Modeling

To model a sculpture, the artist takes a softish material, such as clay, and **molds** it with their hands or using tools. When the final shape is made, texture can be added by pressing shapes into the model or cutting into it with other tools. This structure is fired (baked) or allowed to dry, so that it sets hard. Sculptures can be modeled from many materials including plaster, papier mâché, wax, and bent wire. A completed model can be left as it is or finished off with decoration, such as paint.

Casting

Casting means to make a sculpture using a mold. This is a little like the way you make Jello in a mold. **Cast** sculptures are usually made from **bronze**, steel, or plastic. In the "lost wax" method, an object is made of wax and coated in clay. When the clay is fired, the wax melts and is drained off, leaving an exact impression of the object in the hardened clay, which is then filled with molten (melted) metal. The metal cools and hardens and the sculpture is finished.

◄ *Look at the detail in this warrior's face and costume. The panel, or **plaque**, was cast from bronze using the lost wax method over 200 years ago in West Africa.*

Constructing

Constructed sculptures are made from different materials combined and joined together to form a three-dimensional object. The pieces can be joined in a variety of ways, including gluing, nailing, taping, or even tying together. Metal constructions might be welded (melted) together. Constructed sculptures can be made from new materials, or found materials and junk. Some sculptures are made from reclaimed materials, such as old CDs and washing machine parts!

Ruler of All Egypt

The Great Temple of **Pharoah** (King) Ramesses II was carved from a mountain overlooking the River Nile, Egypt, over 3,000 years ago. Each giant statue is of the pharoah seated on a throne decorated with gods of the Nile. He built the **temple** to worship but also to show how important he was. The statues show that Ramesses was a mighty and powerful ruler of all Egypt.

▼ *Ramesses II*
1225 BC
65 ft. high x 115 ft.
wide (20 m x 35 m)
Great Temple of
Abu Simbel, Egypt

The Story Behind the Art

Ramesses was just 15 when he became pharoah. Although inexperienced in ruling, he faced serious challenges almost immediately. The Hittites, who lived in what is now Turkey, attacked Ramesses' armies to try to take over part of the empire. The young ruler was almost trapped and captured in a fierce battle before reinforcements arrived to save the day.

Back home, Ramesses claimed a huge victory and started a publicity campaign to convince his people and everyone else of his greatness. He built many monuments to himself and even inscribed his own name on statues of other rulers!

Privately, he knew he couldn't defeat the Hittites, so signed a peace treaty with them instead. Then he set out on a building program greater than anything ever seen, including the two temples at Abu Simbel for himself and his favorite wife, Nefertiti.

By the time Ramesses died at 93 years of age, he had had many wives and over 100 children. Many of his people fell into deep mourning, because they had been born during his magnificent reign and they thought the world would end without him.

Eye Spy

Ramesses wears the double crown of Upper and Lower Egypt. His young, handsome face is finely carved and his smiling lips are over a yard wide.

Ramesses' mother Tuya, his Chief Wife Nefertiti, and some of his many children can be seen in smaller scale at his feet. Beneath these giant sculptures are carved figures of bound captives.

The temple is dedicated to the sun god Re-Harakhte. He is shown with the head of a falcon. Carvings of baboons at the top of the temple are shown raising their hands in worship of the sun.

The Terracotta Army

The Terracotta Army is a set of life-size sculptures buried with a Chinese **emperor** in 210 BC. The army is made up of over 8,000 clay soldiers, horses, chariots, and buildings. These numerous sculptures were made to help Emperor Shihuang rule another empire in the afterlife. It is thought that it took 700,000 workers and craftsmen 38 years to complete the army. The terracotta Army was discovered in 1974 by local farmers who were digging a water well.

▼ Terracotta Army
210 BC
6–6.5 ft. high
(1.8–1.97 m high)
Xi'an, Northern China

The Story Behind the Art

*Emperor Shihuang united China. He made everyone use the same kind of money and started building the Great Wall of China, which protected the country from armies attacking from the west. However, he was a mean ruler and made many enemies during his life. Shihuang believed after death he would continue to live in a different world. But gods he had angered by his cruelty on earth could attack him there. So Shihuang had a vast terracotta army made, to be buried alongside him in a massive **tomb** after his death. Each soldier was armed and ready to fight for him in the afterlife. Shihuang was such a cruel emperor that he ordered the sculptors working on the project to be buried alive with him, so that no secrets of the tomb could ever be revealed!*

Eye Spy

The soldiers wear outfits ranging from armor and belted tunics, to coats of chain mail and wind-proof caps. The soldiers were probably modeled in clay sections and the parts fired separately before being stuck together.

There are slight differences in the complexions, expressions, ages, hairstyles, and beards of each warrior. Some people think they may have been modeled on living soldiers. Each was originally painted in bright colors, which have now faded to white.

The Elephant-Headed God

Ganesh is a Hindu god with a human body and an elephant's head, and he is important in the Hindu religion. **Hinduism** is a religion that began in Asia over 3,000 years ago. Ganesh is known as the protector, or Remover of Obstacles. People often pray to him when they are starting a new business and they place him at entrances to protect themselves.

▶ Ganesh
Twentieth century
16.5 ft. (5 m) high
Hyderabad, India

The Story Behind the Art

Lord Shiva, the Hindu god of death and destruction, was away at a war. While he was away, his wife the goddess Pavarti gave birth to a son she named Ganesh. She instructed Ganesh to guard the entrance of her rooms and not to allow anyone in. Lord Shiva returned from war earlier than expected. When he tried to enter Pavarti's rooms, Ganesh stopped him. Shiva did not know Ganesh and was enraged by his impudence. Shiva immediately drew his sword and cut off Ganesh's head.

Pavarti came running from her rooms to find Ganesh without his head and she flew into a rage. To make amends, Shiva promised to take the head of the first living thing he found to replace Ganesh's head. The first animal he came across was an elephant, and that is why Ganesh is always shown with an elephant's head.

Eye Spy

Ganesh usually holds a plate or bowl of sweet food in his hand, or sometimes in his trunk. The sweet is a joyful reward because he is successful in seeking truth. Ganesh's belly is fat because of all the sweets—and therefore the wisdom—it contains!

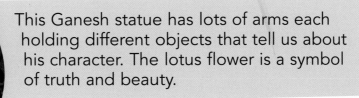

This Ganesh statue has lots of arms each holding different objects that tell us about his character. The lotus flower is a symbol of truth and beauty.

The symbol painted on Ganesh's hand is *om*, or *aum*. In Hindu belief, om is a divine sound. It is the first sound of creation from which life emerged.

Tipu's Tiger

This is Tipu's Tiger, a carved and painted wooden sculpture. It shows a tiger attacking a British soldier. The sculpture was commissioned by Sultan Tipu. Tipu was a king who ruled a large part of southern India with a well-trained army and a fair government. He fought against British forces who were trying to rule India.

Tipu was famous for saying, "Better to live a day as a tiger than a lifetime as a sheep." In other words, he thought it was better to die while being brave and free, rather than to live a long life as a coward, kept by others.

▼ Tipu's Tiger
Eighteenth century
Life-size
Victoria & Albert Museum,
London, England

The Story Behind the Art

Tipu was sultan of Mysore in south India from 1782 to 1799. At this time, Britain already ruled parts of India and was trying to extend its power there. Mysore was one of the most powerful states in India and fought the British with a vengeance.

Tigers and tiger symbols adorned most of Tipu's possessions, from his magnificent throne to the uniforms of his guards. He even had cannons with tigers on and hand weapons decorated with gold tiger heads. Live tigers were kept in the city and there were stories of prisoners thrown into the tiger pits. Tipu thought of himself as a mighty, royal tiger, who was appointed by God to devour God's enemies, the British.

Between 1762 and 1799, there were four Mysore wars. In 1799, the state finally fell to the British and Tipu died fighting bravely in the struggle for the capital city. The British seized many of his belongings as trophies, including the wooden tiger. Eventually, Britain took control of all of India and the country remained under British rule until 1947.

Eye Spy

It is thought that Tipu had this sculpture made around 1790 after hearing a story. A young Englishman out shooting near Calcutta was carried off and killed by an immense tiger. It symbolized Tipu's longed-for defeat of the British, which never came.

When you turn the crank-handle by the tiger's shoulder, it makes a wheezy, roaring sound and the soldier's hand moves up and down. The sounds simulate the growls of the tiger and the cries of its victim!

Raising the Flag of Victory

This statue is a famous war memorial in Washington, D.C., the capital of the United States. It shows one of the most famous incidents of World War II involving the U.S. **Marines**. They fought bravely to take over the Pacific Island of Iwo Jima from Japanese soldiers in 1945. This was an important victory that led to the eventual defeat of Japan. The memorial is dedicated to all the Marines who died defending the United States.

Each marine is over 32 feet (10 meters) tall. Artist Felix de Weldon carved a life-size plaster sculpture based on the real Marines. Then workers at a studio cut it into pieces and used them to create a much bigger version cast in bronze. The parts were made into 12 pieces, some of which weighed over 20 tons. These pieces were transported in trucks to the cemetery where the memorial was to be built. They were then joined together with bolts and melted metal.

▶ The Marine Corps War Memorial
Felix de Weldon
1954
75 ft. (23 m) high
Arlington National Cemetery, Washington, D.C.

UNCOMMON VALOR WAS A COMMON VIRTUE

The Story Behind the Art

By February 1945, U.S. troops had recaptured most of the territory taken by the Japanese in 1941 and 1942 during World War II. However, Japanese forces still held Iwo Jima, a small island south of Japan. On the morning of February 19, 1945, the Marines were ordered to fight and capture Mount Suribachi, a high mountain that makes up the narrow southern tip of the island. Four hard days later, soldiers fighting on the mountain slopes saw a small American flag flying on Mount Suribachi. The sight encouraged them to keep fighting and clear all enemies from the slopes. Then five Marines and a naval medical officer raised a second, larger flag and a newspaper reporter took a photo. This became a famous image back in the United States and was later reproduced as the sculpture.

Eye Spy

The 65.5-ft. (20-meter) flagpole is bronze with a real cloth U.S. flag on top. The same flag flies day and night in permanent tribute to all U.S. Marines who died defending their country.

The positions of the figures show us that the Marines used all their strength and worked together to raise the U.S. flag on Iwo Jima.

Strength of an Eagle

Totem poles are carved and erected by **Native Americans** of the northwest United States and Canada. They are symbols of their family and tribe. Totem poles often tell family histories and stories of the different tribes. This is a Haida Eagle totem pole. The Haida people live on islands on the coast of British Columbia. The stories of the poles are told by parents to their children, so they are remembered year after year.

Animals carved on totem poles are used to represent the different characteristics and strengths of a family or tribe. For example, orca whales are travelers, guardians, and symbols of good, and frogs represent spring and new life.

▶ *Haida Eagle clan totem pole Twentieth century Private collection*

The Story Behind the Art

Historically, the Haida tribe lived along calm and sheltered beaches by forests. They were the most feared coastal North American Indians. The tribe was divided into two clans: the ravens and eagles. It is said the Haida possessed the Eagle's strength and the raven's cunning in battle.

The tribe used tall cedar tree trunks from the forests for many purposes. For example, they built canoes to raid or to trade with nearby tribes. Some canoes were massive—carved from a single cedar tree—and were as long as 15 adults head to toe! The Haida also used the tall cedar tree trunks to make totem poles. They made totems for different reasons, such as to honor the death of a relative. They carved animals and symbols from bottom to top of the totems. The symbols at the bottom were often more finely carved than those at the top, because they were closer to the viewer. Paint to color the totem poles was made from natural products, such as clamshells to make white. The clans raised their totems using ropes and wooden props. Totem-raising was a special event, and often happened during huge parties called potlatches. As they raised the pole, the Haida sang and danced, beat drums and shook rattles. Totems are still made by the Haida people today.

Eye Spy

The thunderbird at the top of this totem pole is a symbol of the Haida tribe. In Haida legends, thunderbirds ruled the sky and occasionally flew to earth to catch whales to eat. When thunderbirds fought massive battles, there was thunder and lightning.

The wolf is shown biting into a fish. Wolves symbolize intelligence and leadership. In Haida legend, wolves also care for their relatives and can heal sickness.

Make a wire sculpture

You will need:

pipe cleaners
• *newspaper* •
masking tape • *glue*
• *paints and
paintbrush*

What you do:

1 Gently bend a pipe cleaner in half. Twist a big loop to form the shape of the head. Twist again farther down and separate the two ends to make legs. Bend ends to make feet.

2 Bend a second pipe cleaner in half and wrap it around the "body" of the first pipe cleaner to make arms. Bend the ends to make hands.

Top Tip!
It's fun to take a digital photograph of someone in a pose so that you can copy it when you're making your sculpture!

3 Bend the body so that it is dancing or even doing a headstand! Standing your figure up may be difficult unless you give it big feet!

22

4 Tape scrunched-up bits of newspaper together to fill the head. Wrap strips of newspaper around the body, arms, and legs to add padding. Check that your figure balances as you go along, since you may need to make adjustments while you are adding the newspaper.

5 Then cover the whole figure with small pieces of newspaper stuck on with glue. This will help make the figure strong and cover any remaining bits of pipe cleaner.

6 When this is dry, you can paint the figure.

You can experiment with decorating your wire sculpture in other materials. Why not cover it with aluminum foil to make it look like silver? Or create a brushed bronzed effect by covering the wire with plaster of Paris, painting it black first, and then with bronze-colored paint. Finally, rub some of the paint off.

Sculpt figures

Here are two ways of making figures.

Clay people

What you do:

1 Take a lump of air-drying clay and start to mold the shape of your figure. Try to make your figure out of one piece of clay and avoid making standing figures, since these may break.

You will need:
air-drying clay
• some tools such as an old fork, a knife, a spoon, and a lollipop stick • poster paints and paintbrush

Top Tip!
Think about what positions you like to relax in, such as lying down cross-legged or sitting with your knees raised up. Practicing these positions will help you to sculpt a realistic figure.

2 Use tools to model and make marks in the figure.

3 When your sculpture has dried out, paint it with poster paint.

Salt dough sculpting

What you do:

1 Plan the design for your sculpture on paper. Maybe you could use an animal design?

Recipe for salt dough

Mix 1 cup of salt and 2 cups of white flour together in a bowl. Then, slowly add 1 cup of hot water (from the tap) and hand kneed the dough until it feels elastic. If the mix is too sticky, add more flour. If it's too dry, add more water.

2 Roll out the salt dough about ½ in. (1 cm) deep. Place your template from step 1 on top of salt dough. Cut out shape with a blunt knife.

Top Tip! Place waxed paper underneath the dough so that it is easier to transfer to a cookie tray later on.

3 Add details to your sculpture using the tools. If you want to create a layered effect, stick pieces of dough to it using a little water.

4 Carefully place the sculpture on a cookie tray and ask an adult to put it in the oven on a low temperature for approximately an hour. Test that it is fired (baked) hard all the way through using a toothpick.

5 When the sculpture has cooled, paint and decorate it.

Make a totem pole

You could create a totem pole that represents your family history. Think of some animals or symbols that represent your family. Maybe your mother is like a wise owl and your little brother is like a puppy dog?

What you do:

1 Measure the paper towel tube's height and width with a ruler. Trim a piece of paper to the same size, allowing a $1/2$ in. (1 cm) overlap around the tube to glue the edges together.

You will need:
sugar paper
• paper towel tube
• ruler • colored pencils, paint, or markers • brown paper
• safety scissors
• glue stick

2 On the sugar paper, draw and color in three or four different animal heads in the center, one above the other. These will go at the front of the totem pole.

3 Wrap and glue the paper around the tube. Make sure you glue the seam firmly at the back.

4 Draw pairs of wings or arms for each of the animals on another piece of paper. Decorate them and cut them out.

5 Glue them to the back of the totem pole.

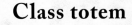

Class totem

If your class wants to make a totem pole, you could work in groups to model several more clay animal faces, and paint and fire them in a kiln (oven). These could be attached one on top of the other on a tall piece of wood to make a totem pole that can cheer up a corner of your school playground!

Glossary

bronze   Metal made by mixing copper and tin. It is good for making sculptures because it does not rust.

carve   To cut by removing the surface of a piece of material.

cast   To make a shape, such as a sculpture, using a shaped mold.

construct   To put together using different parts.

emperor   Powerful ruler of a country, its government, and its army.

Hinduism   Major religion in India and other parts of the world. Hindus believe in many gods and think that their soul is reborn in a new body after death

Marine   A type of U.S. soldier who serves both on land and at sea.

model   To form using clay or other soft material.

mold   Hollow shape used to produce a sculpture.

Native American   Person with ancestors who were the original inhabitants of North America before European settlers arrived.

pharoah   Ancient Egyptian king.

plaque   Flat panel sculpture where modeled shapes stick out from the background.

symbol   Object, figure, or character that represents something else, such as an idea or belief.

temple   Place of worship.

three-dimensional   Something with height, width, and depth.

tomb   Grave or monument to dead people.

totem pole   Large, wooden sculpture with symbols of certain Native American peoples.

tribe   Group of people related by birth and sharing the same language and culture.

Find out more

Books to read

Clay (Artists at Work) by Cheryl Jakab (Smart Apple Media, 2007)
Clay Modelling (Step-by-Step) by Greta Speechley (Heinemann, 2000)
Sculpture (Directions in Art) by Jillian Powell (Heinemann, 2004)
Sculpture (Let's Start Art) by Sue Nicholson (QEB Publishing, 2005)
Sculpture: Three Dimensions in Art (Artventure) by Anne Civardi (Smart Apple Media, 2005)
Stone (Artists at Work) by Cheryl Jakab (Smart Apple Media, 2007)
World Art by Sue Nicholson (Two-Can Publishing, 2006)
Wood (Artists at Work) by Cheryl Jakab (Smart Apple Media, 2007)

Websites to visit

Due to the changing nature of Internet links, PowerKids Press has developed an online list of Web sites related to the subject of this book. This site is updated regularly. Please use this link to access this list:
www.powerkidslinks.com/sia/sculpt

Places to go

New Orleans Museum's City Park, New Orleans, has a collection of over 50 contemporary and modern sculptures.

Seattle Art Museum's Olympic Sculpture Park, Seattle, is a large, green space for displaying art.

Socrates Sculpture Park, Long Island City, New York has an interesting collection of contemporary works.

The Hirshhorn Museum and Sculpture Garden, Washington DC, has a sculpture garden featuring work by Auguste Rodin and Alexander Calder.

The Metropolitan Museum of Art, New York has a fascinating collection of ancient and contemporary sculptures.

The Noguchi Museum, New York, has an extensive collection of the works of the Japanese-American sculpture Noguchi. It includes sculptures in stone, metal, wood and clay.

Index

Photos or pictures are shown below in bold, **like this**.